CW00539118

Wartime Collection

23 classic songs for keyboard

© International Music Publications Ltd
First published in 1996 by International Music Publications Ltd
International Music Publications Ltd is a Faber Music company
Bloomsbury House 74–77 Great Russell Street London WC1B 3DA

Cover Image from Popperfoto/Alamy

Music arranged & processed by Barnes Music Engraving Ltd

Printed in England by Caligraving Ltd
All rights reserved

ISBN10: 0-571-53106-7
EAN13: 978-0-571-53106-6

BLESS 'EM ALL

Words and Music by Jimmy Hughes and Frank Lake

Suggested Registration: Accordian
Rhythm: Waltz
Tempo: ♩ = 176

Bless 'em

all, _____ bless 'em all, _____ the

long and the short and the tall. _____

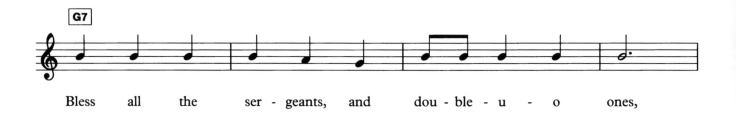

Bless all the ser - geants, and dou - ble - u - o ones,

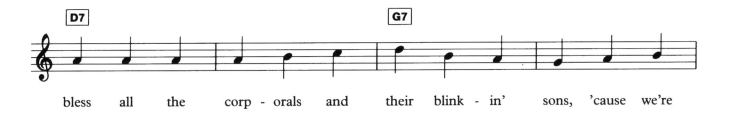

bless all the corp - orals and their blink - in' sons, 'cause we're

say - ing good - bye to them all,_____ as

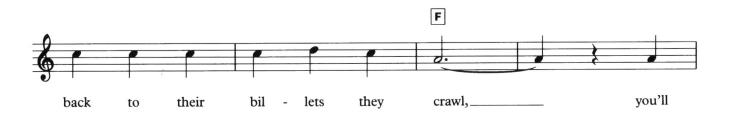

back to their bil - lets they crawl,_____ you'll

get no pro - mo - tion this side of the o - cean, so

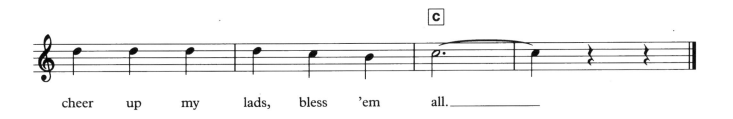

cheer up my lads, bless 'em all._____

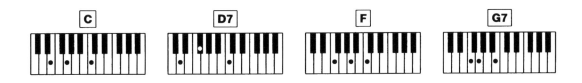

Coming Home

Words and Music by Billy Reid

Suggested Registration: Clarinet
Rhythm: Swing
Tempo: ♩ = 176

Com - ing home,_____ my dar - ling,_____

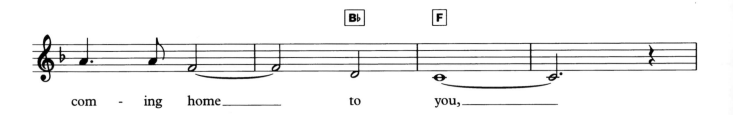

com - ing home_____ to you,_____

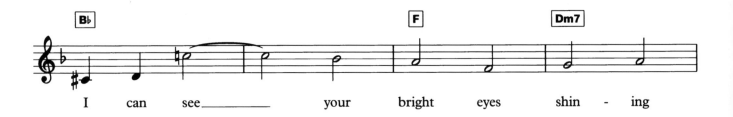

I can see_____ your bright eyes shin - ing

in the clouds._____ There's a sil - ver lin - ing

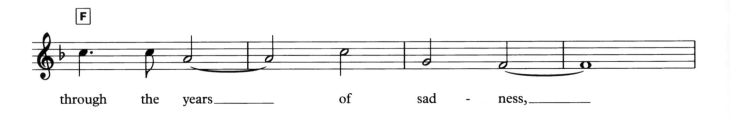

through the years_____ of sad - ness,_____

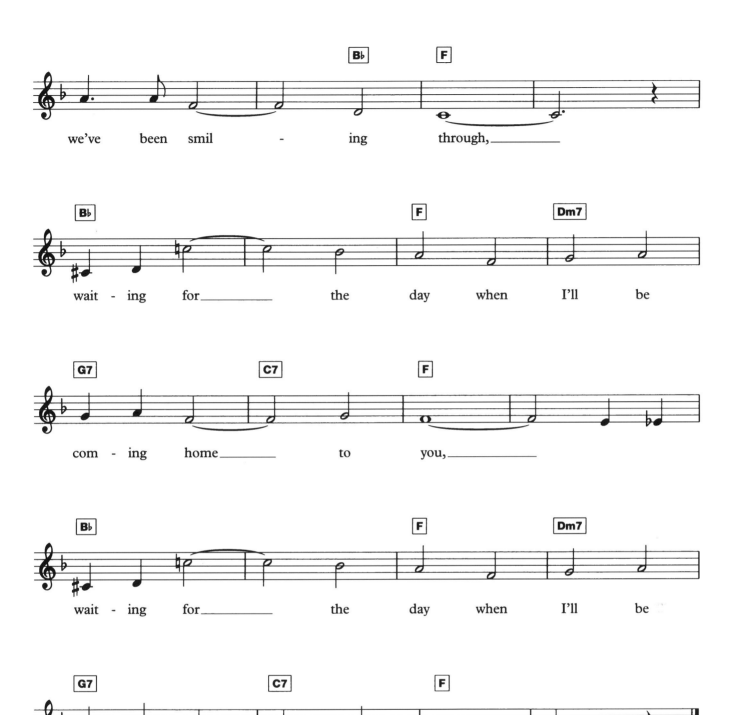

we've been smil - ing through, _____

wait - ing for _____ the day when I'll be

com - ing home _____ to you, _____

wait - ing for _____ the day when I'll be

com - ing home _____ to you. _____

COMRADES

Words and Music by Felix McGlennon

Suggested Registration: Saxophone
Rhythm: Waltz
Tempo: ♩ = 144

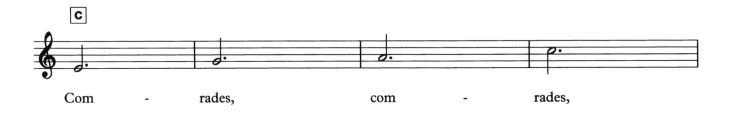

Com - rades, com - rades,

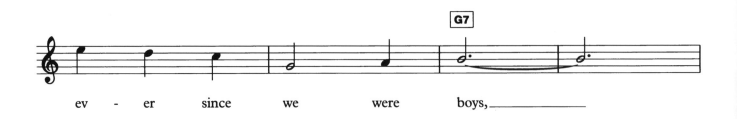

ev - er since we were boys,_____

shar - ing each oth - er's sor - rows,

7

Goodbye Dolly Gray

Words by Will D Cobb / Music by Paul Barnes

Suggested Registration: French Horn
Rhythm: March
Tempo: ♩ = 104

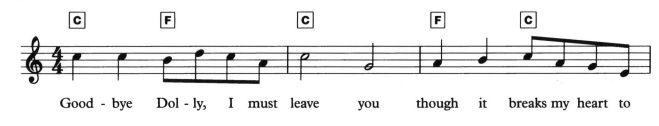

Good - bye Dol - ly, I must leave you though it breaks my heart to

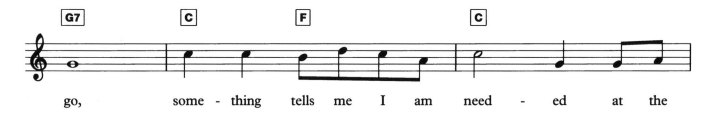

go, some - thing tells me I am need - ed at the

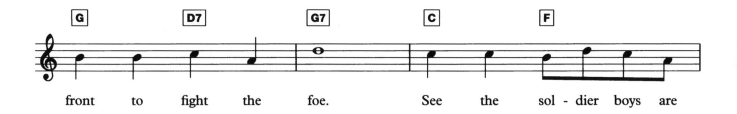

front to fight the foe. See the sol - dier boys are

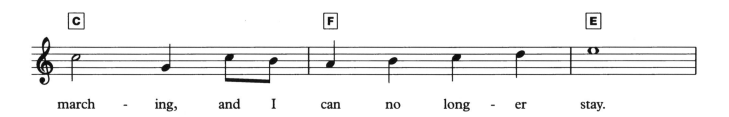

march - ing, and I can no long - er stay.

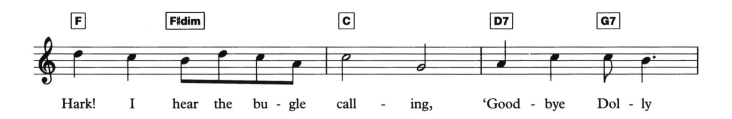

Hark! I hear the bu - gle call - ing, 'Good - bye Dol - ly

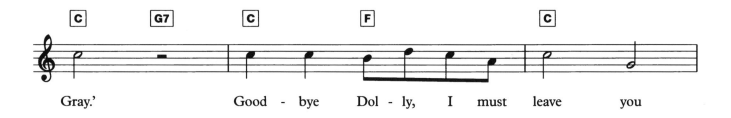

Gray.' Good - bye Dol - ly, I must leave you

GOODBYE-EE!

Words and Music by R P Weston and Bert Lee

Suggested Registration: Clarinet
Rhythm: Swing
Tempo: ♩ = 116

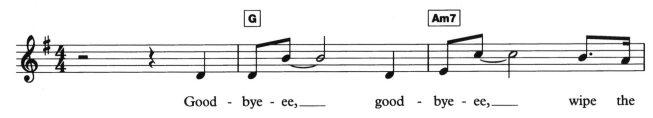

Good - bye - ee,___ good - bye - ee,___ wipe the

tear ba - by dear from your eye - ee,___ though it's hard to part I

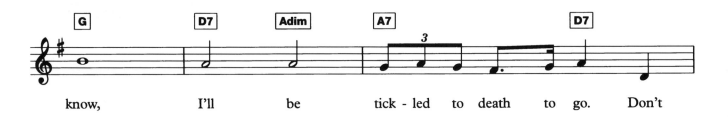

know, I'll be tick - led to death to go. Don't

cry - ee,___ don't sigh - ee,___ there's a sil - ver lin - ing in the

sky - ee.___ Bon - soir old thing, cheer - i - o, chin chin, nah -

-poo too - dle-oo, good - bye - ee!___ Good - bye - ee,___ good -

How Are Things In Glocca Morra?

Words by E Y Harburg / Music by Burton Lane

Suggested Registration: Flute
Rhythm: Soft Rock
Tempo: ♩ = 84

How are things in Gloc - ca Mor - ra?_____ Is that lit - tle brook still

leap - ing there?_____ Does it still run down to Don - ny Cove,_____ through

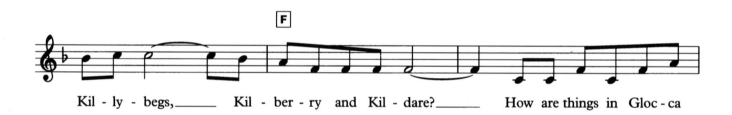

Kil - ly - begs,_____ Kil - ber - ry and Kil - dare?_____ How are things in Gloc - ca

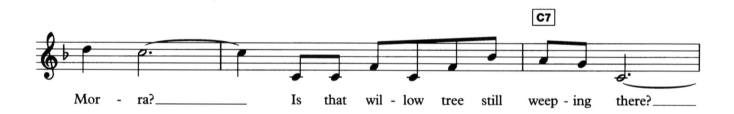

Mor - ra?_____ Is that wil - low tree still weep - ing there?_____

__ Does that lad - die with the twink - lin' eye,_____ come whis - tlin' by,_____ and

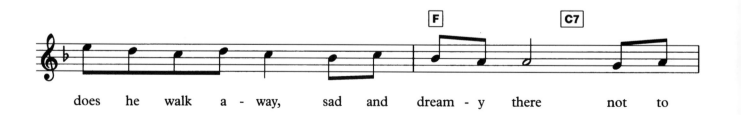

does he walk a - way, sad and dream - y there not to

see me there?_____ So I ask each weep - in'

wil - low, and each brook a - long the way, and each

lad that comes a - whis - tlin', 'Too - ra - lay'._____

___ How are things in Gloc - ca

Mor - ra this fine day?_____

I'll Be Seeing You

Words by Irving Kahal / Music by Sammy Fain

Suggested Registration: Strings
Rhythm: Swing
Tempo: ♩ = 104

I'll be see-ing you___ in all the old fa-

-mi - liar pla - ces that my heart and mind em - brac - es

all day through._____ In that

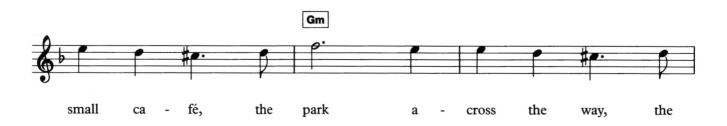

small ca - fé, the park a - cross the way, the

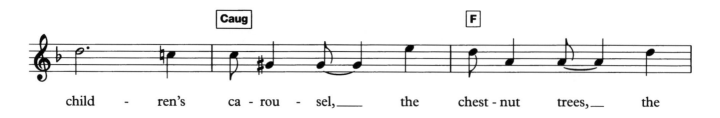

child - ren's ca - rou - sel,___ the chest - nut trees,___ the

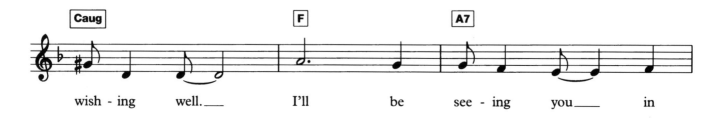

wish - ing well.___ I'll be see - ing you___ in

I'll Close My Eyes

Words and Music by Billy Reid

Suggested Registration: Strings
Rhythm: Rhumba
Tempo: ♩ = 112

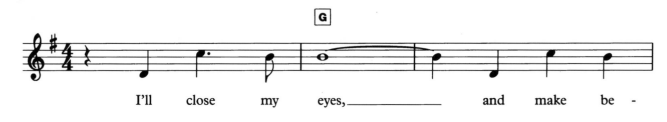

I'll close my eyes, _____ and make be -

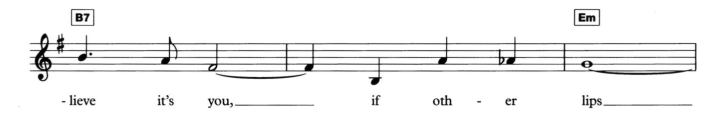

- lieve it's you, _____ if oth - er lips _____

_ should speak of love di - vine, _____ the

stars were mine, _____ but I just reached for the moon, _____

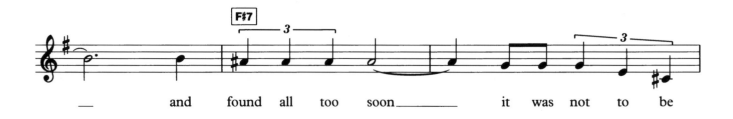

_ and found all too soon _____ it was not to be

mine. _____ I'll close my eyes _____

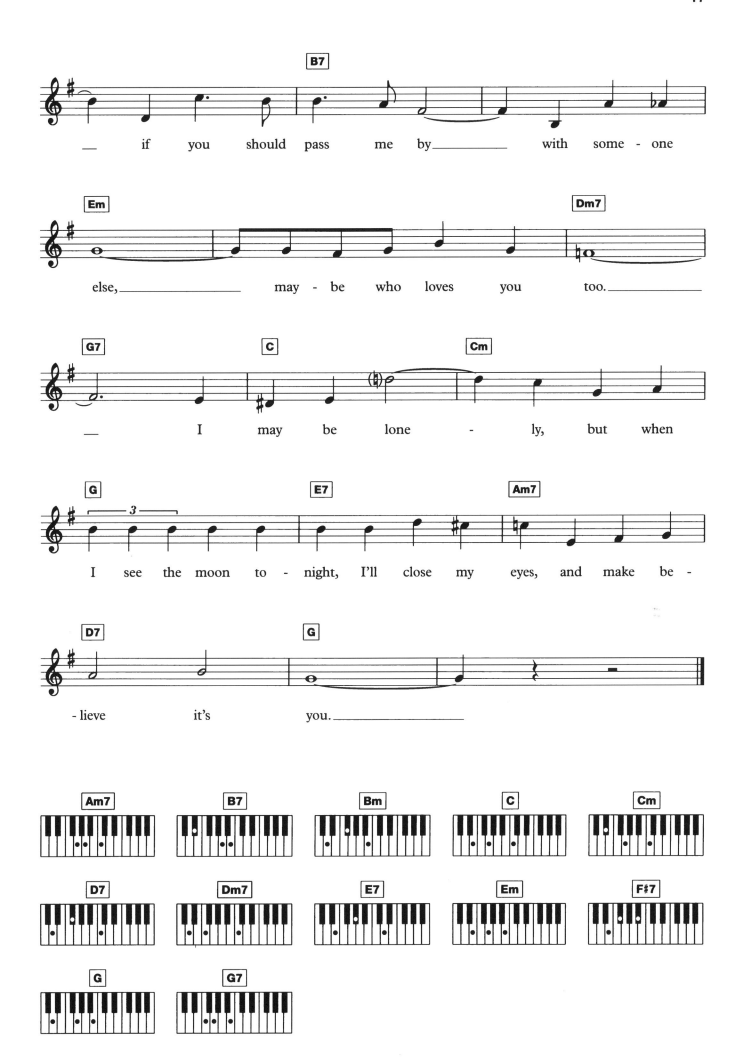

I'll Walk Alone

Words by Sammy Kahn / Music by Jule Styne

Suggested Registration: Vibraphone
Rhythm: Slow Swing
Tempo: ♩ = 104

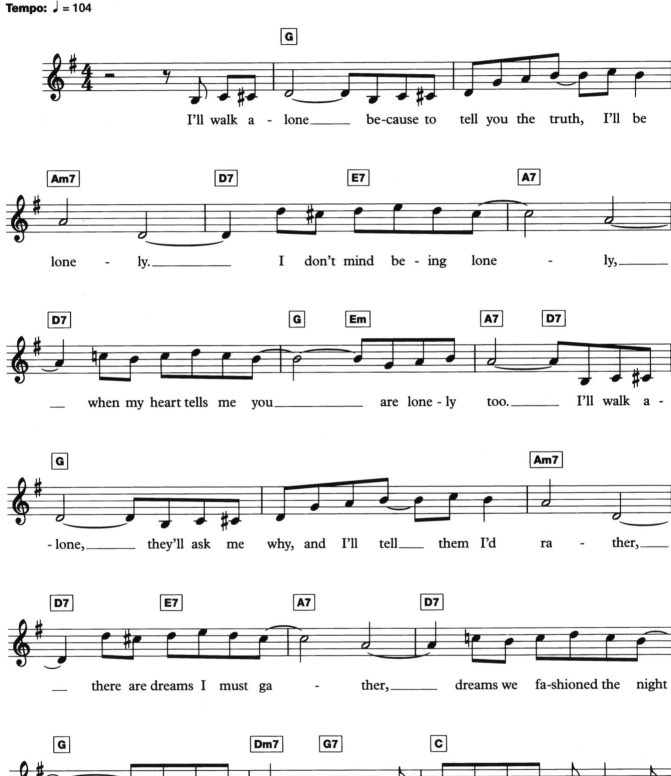

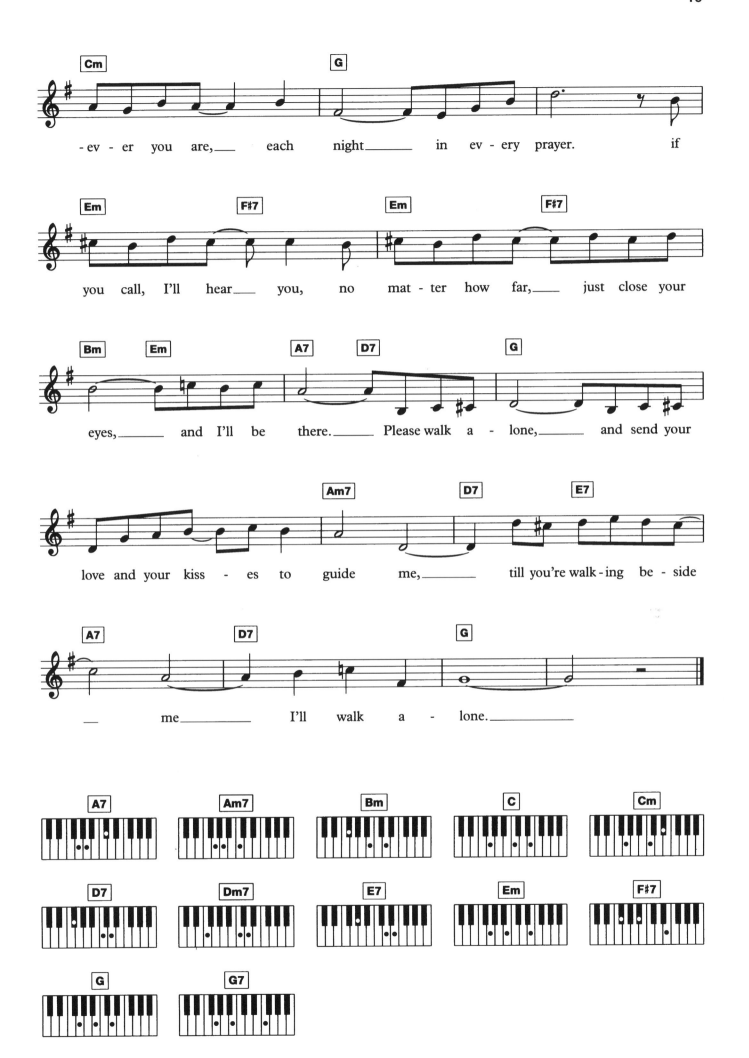

I'm Going To Get Lit-up
(When The Lights Go Up In London)

Words and Music by Hubert Gregg

Suggested Registration: Clarinet
Rhythm: Swing
Tempo: ♩ = 144

lights go up in Lon - don,_____ we'll all be

lit up as the Strand was, on - ly more, much

more, and be - fore the par - ty's played out, they will

fetch the fire bri - gade out to the lit - test up - pest

scene you ev - er saw._____

I'VE GOT A GAL IN KALAMAZOO

Words by Mack Gordon / Music by Harry Warren

Suggested Registration: Saxophone
Rhythm: Swing
Tempo: ♩ = 116

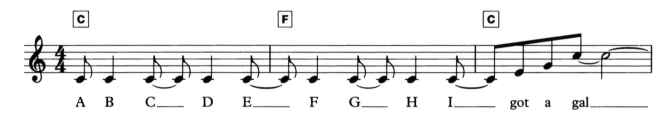

A B C D E F G H I got a gal

in Ka - la - ma - zoo, don't wan-na boast, but I know

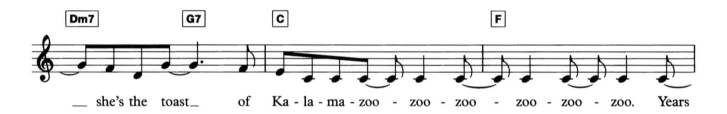

she's the toast of Ka - la - ma - zoo - zoo - zoo - zoo - zoo - zoo. Years

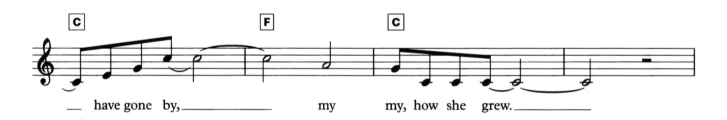

have gone by, my my, how she grew.

I liked her looks when I car - ried her books in Ka - la - ma - zoo - zoo - zoo-

- zoo - zoo. I'm gon - na send a wire, hop-pin' on a fly - er

23

In The Mood

Words and Music by Joe Garland

Suggested Registration: Tenor Saxophone
Rhythm: Swing
Tempo: ♩ = 120

Who's the liv-in' dol-ly with the beau-ti-ful eyes? What a pair o' lips, I'd like to

try 'em for size.__ I'll just tell her, 'Ba-by, won't you swing it with me?'__

Hope she tells me may-be, what a wing it will be.__ So I said po-lite-ly, 'Dar-lin',

may I in-trude?' She said, 'Don't keep me wait-ing when I'm in the mood.'

First I held her light-ly, and we start-ed to dance, then I held her tight-ly, what a

dream-y ro-mance, and I said, 'Hey ba-by, it's a quart-er to three,

25

It's A Long Way To Tipperary

Words and Music by Jack Judge and Harry Williams

Suggested Registration: French Horn
Rhythm: March
Tempo: ♩ = 120

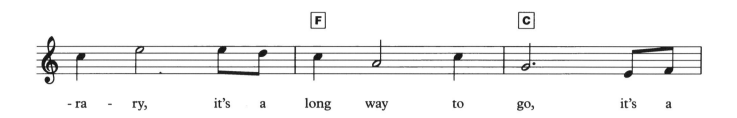

-ra - ry, it's a long way to go, it's a

long way_____ to Tip - pe - ra - ry, to the sweet - est girl I

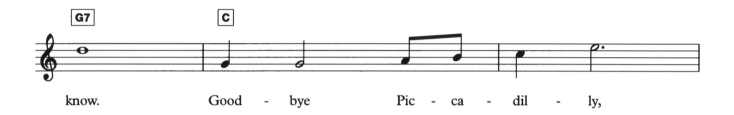

know. Good - bye Pic - ca - dil - ly,

fare - well Leic - ester Square, it's a long long way to Tip - pe -

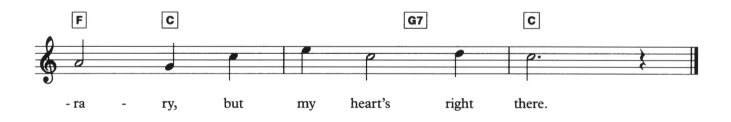

-ra - ry, but my heart's right there.

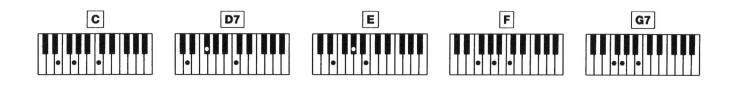

Jolly Good Luck To The Girl Who Loves A Soldier

Words by Fred W Leigh / Music by Kenneth Lyle

Suggested Registration: Flute
Rhythm: 6/8 March
Tempo: ♩ = 96

Jol - ly good luck to the girl who loves a sol - dier,

girls,_____ have you been there?_____

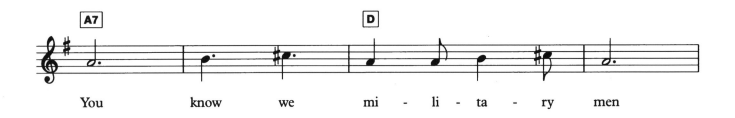

You know we mi - li - ta - ry men

al - ways do our du - ty ev - ery - where.____

Jol - ly good luck to the girl who loves a sol - dier,

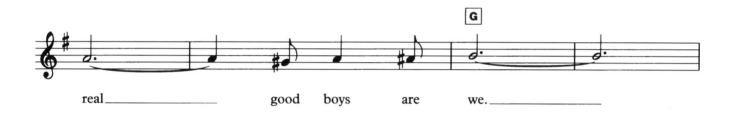

real____ good boys are we.____

Girls, if you'd like to love a sol - dier, you can

all love me.____

Now Is The Hour

Words by Maewa Kaihau / Music by Clement Scott

Suggested Registration: Strings
Rhythm: Waltz
Tempo: ♩ = 116

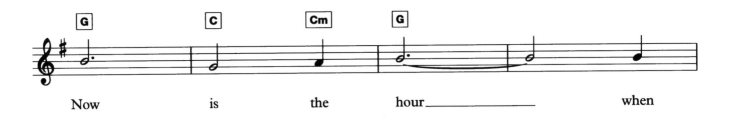

Now   is   the   hour_____   when

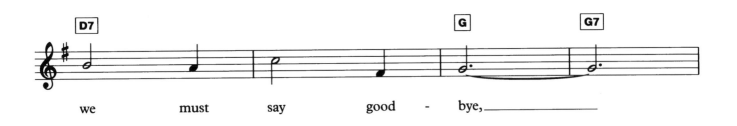

we   must   say   good - bye,_____

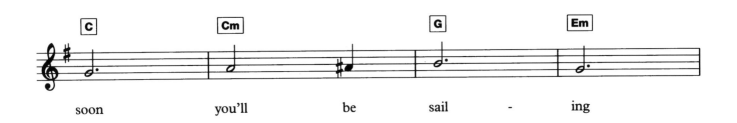

soon   you'll   be   sail -   ing

Soldiers Of The Queen

Words and Music by Leslie Stuart

Suggested Registration: French Horn
Rhythm: March
Tempo: ♩ = 112

Bri - tons al - ways loy - al - ly de - claim a - bout the way we rule the

waves, ev - ery Bri - ton's song is just the same when

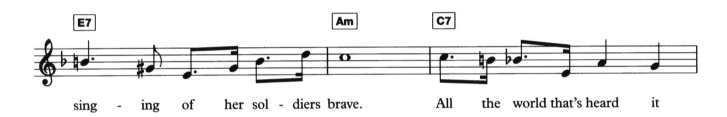

sing - ing of her sol - diers brave. All the world that's heard it

won - ders why we sing, some have learned the rea - son why.

We're not for - get - ting it, we're not let - ting it

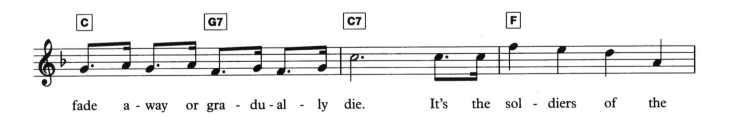

fade a - way or gra - du - al - ly die. It's the sol - diers of the

Queen, my lad, who've been, my lads, who've seen, my lads, in the

fight for Eng - land's glo - ry lads, it's Eng - land's sol - diers of the

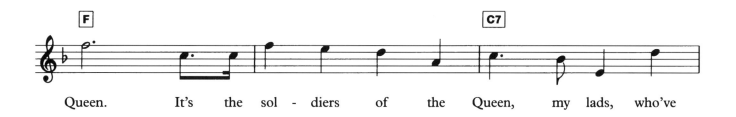

Queen. It's the sol - diers of the Queen, my lads, who've

been, my lads, who've seen, my lads, in the fight for Eng - land's

glo - ry lads, it's Eng - land's sol - diers of the Queen.

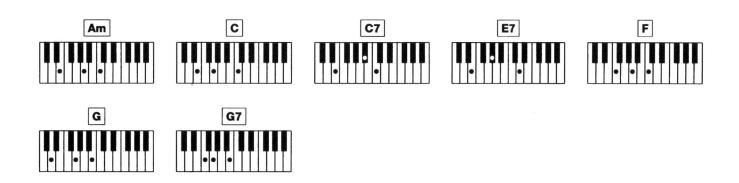

SOMEWHERE IN FRANCE WITH YOU

Words and Music by Michael Carr

Suggested Registration: Flute
Rhythm: Waltz
Tempo: ♩ = 112

There are two eyes, such blue eyes a - smil - ing at me, yet they're love - ly as on - ly a wo - man's can

be, for I see all her thoughts are some -

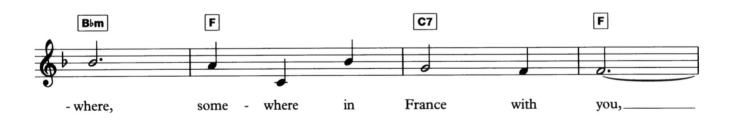

- where, some - where in France with you,_____

___ and when your let - ters come, they bring a smile, a

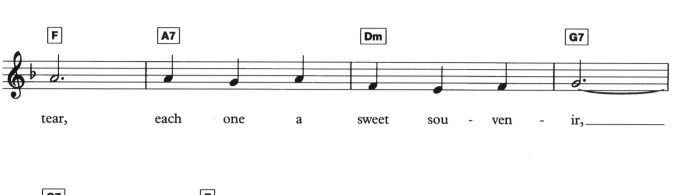

tear,   each   one   a   sweet   sou - ven - ir,_____

___   on - ly   one   of   a   mil - lion   who'll   ne - ver   com -

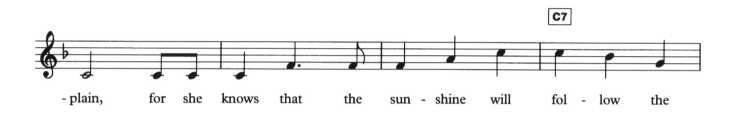

- plain,   for   she   knows   that   the   sun - shine   will   fol - low   the

rain.   Ev - ery   beat   of   her   heart   will   al - ways

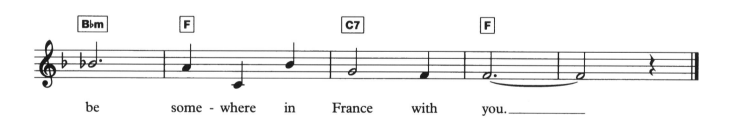

be   some - where   in   France   with   you._____

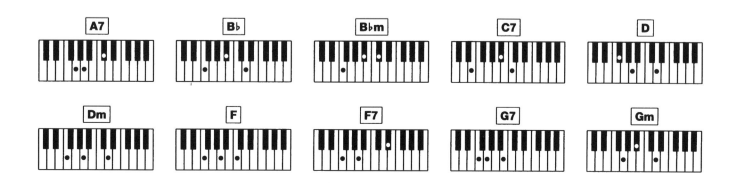

TAKE ME BACK TO DEAR OLD BLIGHTY

Words and Music by A J Mills, Fred Godfrey and Bennett Scott

Suggested Registration: Clarinet
Rhythm: 6/8 March
Tempo: ♩. = 112

Take me back to dear old

Bligh - ty, put me on the

train for Lon - don town._____

Take me o - ver there, drop me a - ny -

- where, Li - ver - pool, Leeds or Bir - ming - ham, well

There'll Always Be An England

Words and Music by Ross Parker and Hughie Charles

Suggested Registration: French Horn
Rhythm: March
Tempo: ♩ = 92

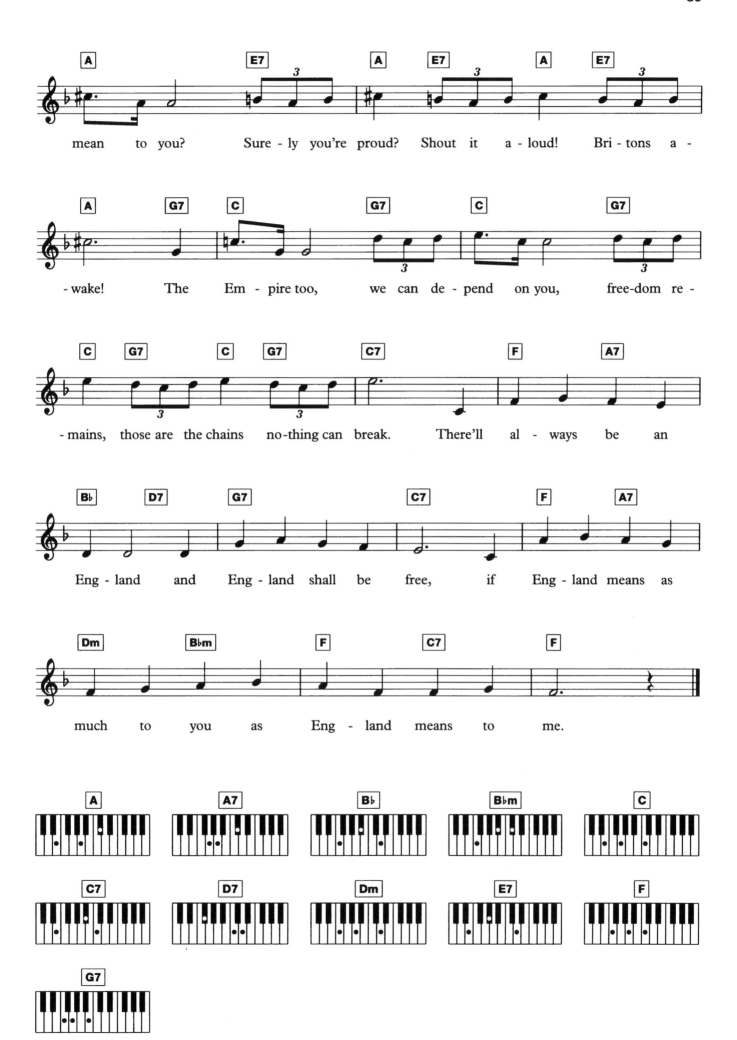

39

WE'LL GATHER LILACS

Words and Music by Ivor Novello

Suggested Registration: Flute
Rhythm: Swing
Tempo: ♩ = 128

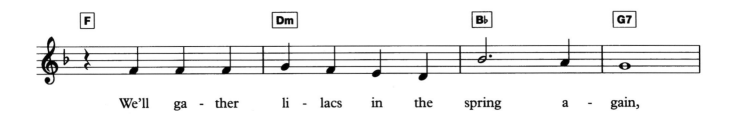

We'll ga - ther li - lacs in the spring a - gain,

and walk to - ge - ther down an Eng - lish lane,

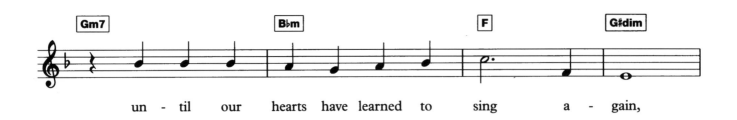

un - til our hearts have learned to sing a - gain,

when you come home once more,_____

and in the eve - ning, by the fire - light's glow,

you'll hold me close, and ne - ver let me go.

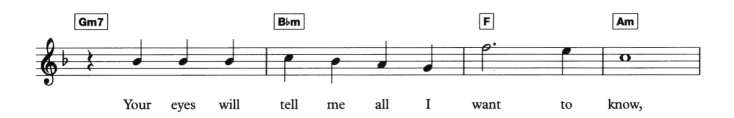

Your eyes will tell me all I want to know,

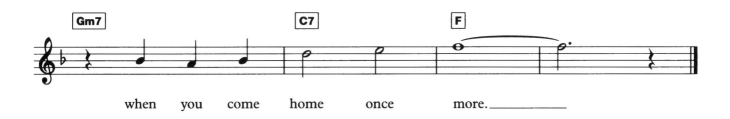

when you come home once more._____

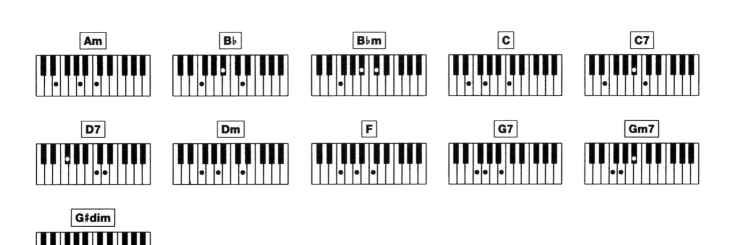

WE'LL MEET AGAIN

Words and Music by Ross Parker and Hughie Charles

Suggested Registration: Vibraphone
Rhythm: Swing
Tempo: ♩ = 96

folks that I know, tell them I won't be long,_____ they'll be

hap - py to know_ that as you saw me go___ I was sing - ing this

song. We'll meet a - gain, don't know

where, don't know when, but I know we'll meet a -

- gain some sun - ny day._____

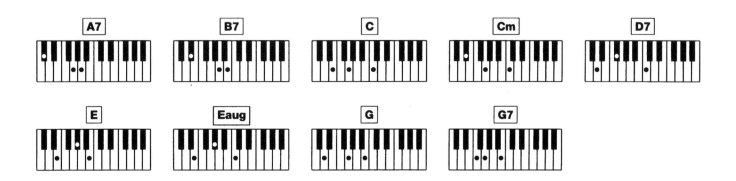

Your King And Country Want You

Words and Music by Paul A Rubens

Suggested Registration: French Horn
Rhythm: March
Tempo: ♩ = 112

Oh! We don't want to

lose you, but we think you ought to go, for your

King and your coun - try both need you

so. We shall want you and miss you, but with

all our might and main, we shall cheer you, thank you,

YOURS

Words by Augustin Rodriguiez / Sub-author Jack Sherr / Music by Gonzalo Roig

Suggested Registration: Strings
Rhythm: Swing
Tempo: ♩ = 144

Yours, till the stars lose their glo - ry,____

__ yours, till the birds fail to sing.____

Yours, to the end of life's sto - ry,____

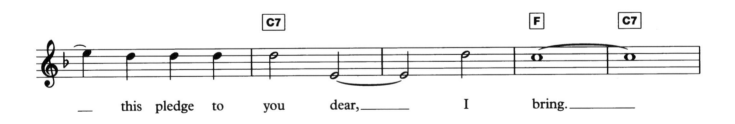

__ this pledge to you dear,____ I bring.____

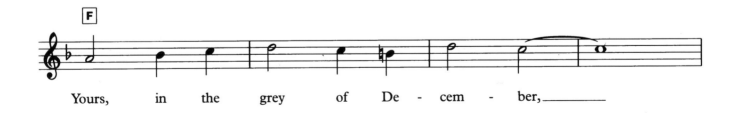

Yours, in the grey of De - cem - ber,____

here or on far dis - tant shores,_____

I've ne - ver loved a - ny - one the way___ I love

you, how could I when I was

born to be_____ just yours?_____

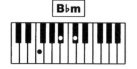
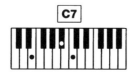
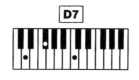
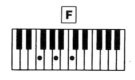
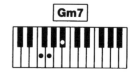

Printed and bound in Great Britain

The Easy Keyboard Library

An expansive series of over 50 titles!

Each song features melody line, vocals, chord displays, suggested registrations and rhythm settings.

"For each title ALL the chords (both 3 finger and 4 finger) used are shown in the correct position – which makes a change!"
Organ & Keyboard Cavalcade

Each song appears on two facing pages,
eliminating the need to turn the page during performance.

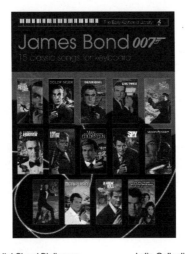

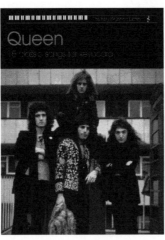

To buy Faber Music publications or to find out about the full range of titles available
please contact your local music retailer or Faber Music sales enquiries:

Faber Music Ltd, Burnt Mill, Elizabeth Way, Harlow CM20 2HX
Tel: +44 (0) 1279 82 89 82   Fax: +44 (0) 1279 82 89 83
sales@fabermusic.com   fabermusic.com   expressprintmusic.com